The Years
That Were

Sia Isa

First published in the UK in 2024

Text © Sia Isa 2023
Cover and inside illustrations © Sia Isa 2023

All rights reserved.
No part of this publication may be reproduced, distributed, or transmitted in any form by any means, including photocopying, recording, or other electronic methods without the prior written permission of the author, except in the case of brief quotations embodied in reviews and certain other noncommercial uses permitted by copyright law. For permission requests, please contact the author at: sia.isa@gmail.com

A CIP catalogue record for this book is available from
the British Library

ISBN 978-1-7392336-9-3

Printed and bound in Great Britain

This book is dedicated to all those who care

Contents

1. Preface 6
2. Bleeding Palestine 8
3. Covid Times 30
4. Tribulations of Inclusivity 42
5. Football & Hooligans 52
6. The Government 60
7. Film & Media 72
8. Digital Addiction & Suffering 82
9. Climate Catastrophe 98
10. The Eejits 106
11. The People 118

Preface

The turmoil in Palestine, coupled with incidents occurring between 2020 and 2021, such as George Floyd's murder, COVID-19 and other important topics such as climate change, the government, the digital world and more, encouraged the writing that is included in this book. This has been my avenue to vent and rant about what I feel is important. However, I never published this book until 2024, as the atrocities thereafter, in Palestine, pulled at my heart strings. I lost confidence in my writing, and pain just sat deep within, with no words spewing out. But it's halfway through this year, that I feel the need to share this. I managed to only write a few pieces about the carnage and utter annihilation of the Palestinian people today. Please note, of course my heart goes out to the many Israelis who lost their lives, which then set the course of devastation and destruction of the innocent souls in Palestine. My heart bled and still bleeds as we see no resolve, just evil unleashed on innocent victims, a large proportion, children and babies being killed every day. A newfound hell on earth

I collated this collection of the spoken word from my Instagram account and published them in this book. I haven't asked anyone to proofread, or copy edit this, nor does the writing follow any particularities of poetry. The writing flowed as words sprung quickly and if I had thought too much about the structure, the essence of what was trying to be conveyed, would be lost swiftly. And for some critics already, the spoken word or poetry does not need to rhyme.

But please note, these poems are not for everyone and may be deemed too controversial. There will be Tory fans, Zionists, Covid conspiracists, the film world and more, that may disagree with my verbatim, but we live in a world (well some of us), where freedom of speech exists, and we are all entitled to our opinion. As I write in one of my poems 'we are different grains in the sand…passing through this lawn'. And it's only through having a different opinion, does the world move along. If you are offended too much, feel free to stop reading or try another topic. I am not expecting everyone to have the same perspective of the world as I do, but I also ask that sometimes putting oneself in the shoes of another, can open one's mind to a multitude of understanding from that person's perspective. But again, this may not be for everyone. Peace!

Bleeding Palestine

It's because of the events in Palestine in 2021, that my Instagram page started formation. I wanted to know where all this conflict stemmed from, and learnt that the trials and tribulations of the Palestinian people started way back in the early 1900s by the UK Prime minister of that time. It is this man of the name Balfour, who should be held culpable for the signed document, whose declaration in 1917 caused what is still a divide now. May you rest in peace Mr Balfour, whilst the people whose land you taketh away and gifted to another, find no peace.

The collection of poems here touch on reality, a dream, the nightmare and more, including the evil unleashed after October 7th 2023.

Massacres

It was happening again
The news said it was a massacre
Oh no, not again. Why disturb the peace
We had so been assuming

Now I really don't care for the vigilantes
They may think they are doing right
But killing civilians?
Who put you on earth to go against the Almight?

Now look what happened
You disturbed the big bully
The settlers who stole a land
When the people were so giving

But the settlers had been so moulded
From the Nazi war crime, their ancestors had so lived in
Let's go break the law
Of humanity and any UN sanction put in

And so, they unleashed a torment
That Hitler and Stalin would be so proud of
Sent carnage to those innocent
Killed children with no thoughts therein

The world is going to heat up
With anger and torment
Protests and social media has been lit up
Like a bush fire that you can't put out

This is a war crime
From inhumane minds
Wow Satan would be proud
That his disciples are doing his work with no restraint

Yes it was happening again
But this was worse than all
Innocent victims being killed and tormented
By the devil's army and so many more

Politicians sat twiddling
Not thumbs, but each other's family jewels
Sending aid to help the oppressors
Not a thought for the ones they savaged

The worldly leaders have become futile
No conscience of their actions
Civilians have anger spewing rebuke
Of the injustice that is invoked on the masses

Nothing makes sense anymore
Wild animals probably would make better rulers
They would show some humanity
Than the recent animals we've had to endure

Arthur James Balfour

Oh Arthur James Balfour
What did you do?
You wrote a declaration
For a land, you had no due

Destiny altered
A homeland destroyed
Hundred years or so ago
A decision so poor

Now only a handful of MPs show tiny remorse
Whilst you lie at Whittinghame
A war brews and continues
An unfair, one-sided form of bullying

Imposing limits and rules
Refugee camps, a wall
No regard for the natives
Almost like the Nazi camps repeating

Oh the majesty's government
You have yet to take that moral responsibility
Of yet another decision
That has led to today's reality

Picture This

Picture the town, city or village you live in
Picture it peaceful, living shoulder to shoulder
With Jim, Catherine, Muhammad or Mary

Picture a man, in a faraway land
Making decisions on behalf of your clan
Not holding ownership or any kind of connection
Sending the refugees to move into your habitation

Picture you not sure, but it will have to be
To avoid being unjust
Sometimes you get on
Sometimes not so much

Picture disagreements
And physical exchanges
And that for years and years
The old story remaining

Now picture this story
One hundred years old
And that in 1948
The refugees overtook to unfold

Renamed the land that you once lived in
Put you instead in a tiny little settlement
Built a wall and imposed all sanctions
Beat you up, to show their ranking

Picture now, pulling you from the place you dwell in
Where your father and forefathers lived, and were bore in
Picture you getting angry
For human emotion is a natural instinct

Picture you being beaten
Because you have tried, tried to defeat them
Picture this unjust and unruly place
Like your house with some guests, stealing what you inherited

An Orphan Am I

Who will call my name in the morning
Tell my eight year old self to wake up
Baba please come back
You have years to be my dad

Who will tell me to shut the door
Or play football with me outside
Baba please say something
You have years to be my dad

Who will take me in their arms
When I've fallen or feeling sad
Baba please hug me now
You have years to be my dad

Who will wake me up for dawn prayers
When I can't get up from deep slumber
Baba please wake me up
You have years to be my dad

Who will help me with my homework
Or tell me off when I am slacking
Baba please tell me off
You have years be my dad

Who will tell me to be a good brother
To look after little Aisha, she is only three
Baba tell me how to do that
You have years to be my dad

They killed you in the mosque
They killed them in the hospital
Made us orphans in thousands
Made us so so regrettable
We didn't do anything wrong
We just wanted to play outside
We wanted to have dinner with Mama and Baba
And go to school and learn all things great
We wanted to listen to that story
That Baba told us so carefully
Have lots of laughs, sing melodies
With our dear parents, so affectionately
We just wanted to be children
Live normal children lives
But that was taken away
And we may never ever know, it was our right
We now wait for the day we are reunited
With Mama, Baba, friends and family
Play and rejoice in a place not of this earth
Where destruction and hurt will only be a mere thought

Mama, Hussein, Zahra

Mama, Hussein, Zahra
Where are you?
You told me this morn we would have food
Why are you all not up yet?
It's half past nine
I only put you in the corner, to protect what's mine

Mama, Hussein, Zahra
Talk to me
Why are you not moving under the rubble I see?
Why is it dusty?
The room is usually clean
I know that wall has dropped, and I can see out clearly

Mama, Hussein, Zahra
Come back to me
I need you, I can't live life without you my family
Oh my lord,
I cannot breathe
This pain of sadness will be eternity

Sleep My Child

My dear, dear child, now just go to sleep
But Mother, it's hard, when I hear such loud beeps
Oh that's just the fairies, fighting the warlocks
Oh really Mama? What are they fighting for?

Fighting so that you and I can have lots of peace
But Mama, this is Palestine, there has never been peace
My child, and what do you know of such things?
You my girl, should know of only the fun therein

I know Mama, the sound is a bomb
It's not warlocks or fairies, it's people with big guns
Fighting against us with our pebbles and rocks
I know Yasser's dad has gone back, back to God

Just like his brother and Papa did and some
I know that they want us to leave Mama, this home
Where Grandma, Grandpa were born...our family home
But where will we go Mama? Here is where we belong

That is part of the fighting my dear little girl
Now sleep my darling and I'll see you in the morn
I hope so Mama. I hope so I will
Else, see you in the next world. I will be waiting.

The Holocaust

The holocaust so barbaric
Killed so many Israelites
The trauma and the crimes barbaric
Was a real crushing, heinous time

What did they do to deserve this?
Absolutely nothing at all
Why would the Nazis impose a regime?
Of control and ousting and all

Oh Israelites, I'm sorry
For the ancestral crime
I hope you found peace
In the next generations that came to help your kind

Please don't hold anger
Try and find peace instead in your mind
Be grateful for Balfour and the colonials
Who helped you get out of that place and time

Let you settle in Palestine
A beautiful cultural land
The people were welcoming
Maybe some needed time

Fast forward one hundred years
I cannot believe my eyes
What happened to you O' people?
Did you forget the Nazi crime?

Why is apartheid here?
Imposed on the original clan
Why did you build a wall?
I can't understand your plan

Why are you calling eviction?
On residents that were always there
Why are your men in uniform?
Causing fear and scaremongering everywhere

Why would you do the same as Hitler did?
Did the same to you back then
Surely you haven't forgotten
The torture and oppression, inflicted back then

Let's Play Outside

Come on Yahya
Let's go play outside!
Mama can we play
We won't go over to that side

Be careful out there
She says. It is not safe
Don't go beyond yonder
And stay away from any structure

And off we go
Kick the ball Moosa!
Yay! I'm going to be the next Ronaldo
I'm going to be Messi! Shouts back Moosa

Let's play with a better ball
Next week, shouts Moosa
I will get my baba
To buy us one just as great

And we can have treats
Have a party, shouts Yahya
We can invite all our friends
To play, it will be great

******

No Moosa, be careful
Moosa! Moosa!
I can't hear anything
Just a pitch sound
And the building falling

It's a blast! Moosa let's get inside
Moosa get up!
Moosa you are covered in dust
But what is that pouring
It's red or brown
Moosa! Your arm!
I cannot see it
Moosa! Your arm!
Is over there
Let me get it
Moosa! Moosa!
Let me get Mama to call the doctor
But I myself cannot move
My leg!
It hurts!
It hurts so badly!

Standing For A Cause

Every week, every day
Stand the people with conviction so grave
Through the means of social media
Through the weapons of placards and banners
Scarves wrapped around
Like shrouds worn by the dead
And pins stuck to show
The blood shed when killed

This needs to stop
The pain, the killings
Government puppets
Help us. Please
We will not rest
Stop these killings
Else what's the difference between a terrorist, serial killer
And Netanyahu's army dread

Absolutely nothing
Only maybe the former two were not right in the head
IDF are relentless
No soul or remorse
For the things they do for their daily bread
They can't be human
Spilling a child's blood, right there in front
How do they sleep?
Like a baby they once killed?

Protestors galore
You bring some reassurance
To the people who need help
Deepest thanks for what you do
Your soul stands for the plight
It's an absolute human duty
You are anti-Zionists, not antisemitic
You are just standing for what needs to be put right

Living Side by Side

There's a cease fire
Let's all go celebrate
For what exactly? I am unsure
Peace? Sincerity?
Are you sure of the integrity

If we live side by side
How beautiful would be that life
Living harmoniously
Rid of arrogance and profanity
Not feeling imprisoned
Behind some wall or IDF vision

Your neighbour, my neighbour
Sharing Eid, Ramadan, Christmas or Hannukah
That would be a dream come true
My house, my family, my life
All safe and proud with you

The Dream

I walked down the road
Through a wall that used to exist
Off to the farmland I go to sow
With no army man to desist

I visited my Nan in Sheikh Jarrah
She'd been living there since 1939
She had access to everything always
And abundant blissful awareness of every kind

When I left, I saw children playing
They had flowers in their hands
Hurling petals at each other
So all the colours they could see blend

Then I went to pray at Al Aqsa
It was so tranquil in there
I stepped outside after prayer
Said salaams to all the people there

Then I walked back to my neighbourhood
With a hop, skip and jump
I pushed open a small wooden gate
That opened to a garden just

We had dinner that evening
As a family we rejoiced
Laughing whilst planning the weekend ahead
And what time to the beach, we would go

Covid Times

The 2020/2021 pandemic will go down in history as one of the most profound, life changing events that unfolded. On an overseas trip in January 2020, I read the headlines of what was happening in China. Not another Bird flu, Swine flu, Ebola kind of virus, I thought. Never did I think it would change our lives forever.

The new normal is what became during and after. Is there an after, as I write this at the end of 2021? Well, it's still going on with variant after variant being introduced.

The Coronavirus felt like a war. So many lives lost, so many lives displaced. But this war was different. There were no demolished buildings, nor a war zone, just the war zone inside of us all. Has this been the epitome of the 21st century?

Covid Belief

Anti vaxxers
Conspiracy theorists
Covid disbelievers
This is for you

The virus was real
Claimed lives in huge deals
Families distraught
Gasping for breath really hurt

So many died
Lots left fighting lingering effects for a while
Masks had to be worn
Let's be courteous and spread not our asymptomatic germs

This was no flu
More of a menace that blew
So please don't deny this as influenza
You haven't a clue

Clearly you didn't get it
Lucky you
Didn't know anyone who fought it
What bubble are you?

Heard of no lives lost
In your periphery
Hence you must think
Whatever you want it to be

I commiserate your naivety
Living in your world must be like gravity
Floating up above the clouds to cloud nine
The depravity of your innocent mind

The Song from China

China has a song out
Covid conceived in Fort Derick! They shout
Timely when some findings are to be unleashed
Are we sitting on the offensive, we speak

But what about the Wuhan Lab Leak?
Did it stop to reach a peak?
Is it just one offing the other?
Will the propaganda do nothing, but smother?

It's hilarious you see
Whatever the theory may be
Let's not forget, a virus existed
And hone in on curing intricacies

Let's look at what can be rectified
Help those displaced, who lost and left to improvise
Put aside the Malthus theory rants
Let's help our humanity to advance

Lockdown Ease

Everyone is getting excited
As the lockdown starts easing

Flights are full to the brim
As holiday makers fill to the rim

Tests are done
And vaccinations some

Some towns still crying
As hospital beds overflowing

A new variant is in town
Will it be lethal and let us down?

This is not a time to be slack
We must abide by rules in tack

Else that fourth lockdown will be here
And we'll be back to something drear

Judgement and Reason

Judgement and Reason sat down one day
The winter of 2020 dwindled on
Judgement and reason there sat by the fire
Reason with a bubbling cup of cocoa.

Judgement:
Happy New Year they said
May it be a great new year they said
And look what happened. Pfff

Reason:
It all happened indeed, my dear friend Judgement
We can look back with cheer

Judgement:
Cheer? Cheer? Hath you gone mad my silly friend?
How could there be cheer?

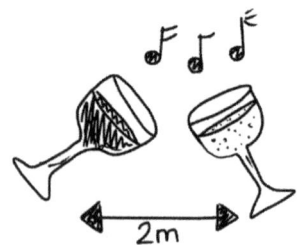

When so many died
So many lost jobs
Many became homeless
Many hit hard with illness of the mental kind
Families left distraught
Not knowing where for food they thought

Couples broke up
Human touch was non existent
There was a recession
There were fights
One spat on a train worker and killed her

There was loneliness, depression
Life got put on hold
No more holidays
Nor ways of finding love
Yet there you are my dear Reason, you say cheer?
What is wrong with you dear Foe!?

Reason:
Listen up crazy Judgement
These you mention did unfold
It was indeed a dark period
But the lining of silver, you never told

The air cleaned up, don't you know
Take it in deep and your lungs will be aglow
Children got to stay at home with their parents and siblings
So much lost time, to make up for

It was a time to sit back, reflect, and take a break
From life's busy mundane chores
Old friends reacquainted
The digital world was busy and more
World's connected, time zones disappeared
Zoom, WhatsApp and the party house app was set on fire
I can tell you more

Food cooked became an interest, not a chore
Exercise was a pursuit not ignored
Nature pulled these humans off their buttocks
It was a refreshing day's ritual; I tell you so

So, there you have it my dear friend judgement
Trialing times of course I know
But silver linings and pretty gems
Paved the path of the year that was 2020

Judgement listened intently and sighed

Judgement:
My oh my dear Reason, that was quite a verbatim you told
Now let me tell you of the human race, that is fatigued and more

Last night there were masses at a metropolis owned
by King Harrod [1]
What a sight
There were street parties held for festive fun, also that night
With wine and carols and children full of delight
It's all good and well to have some festive fun and cheer
But back to being locked they will be, if that third wave is near

Reason
Oh dear, dear Judgement, that may be so
The human spirit is in turmoil, I am sure you know
They were never designed to stay locked in
– it's never good for the soul
So when let out as thirsty cats, they went to fill those bowls

Alas, a cure is here! Have you not been told
The only way is up. It can only get clear
With an elixir injected and wise and clever moves
The world will breathe a fresh again.

---

1 Harrods store in London

Judgement
Well, we shall see, you spirit of reason
Time will only tell
I take my hat and bid you adieu
Let's meet in 2021 and see what unfolds

Reason:
Very well dear Judgement
And a happy 2021. May it be full of merriment and less woe

Judgement walks away into the darkness. Reason sits adding a marshmallow to the inviting cup of cocoa.

Tribulations of Inclusivity

A chapter mainly dedicated to the movement that occurred in 2020 when George Floyd was killed by the knee of who was meant to be an officer of the law. This lit the world up and plenty of people came out to protest about the mistreatment of the black people, prevalent since centuries ago. If this book is being read 100 years after, or even five years later, I hope things have changed immensely and the mere thought of a person of colour being terrorised or mistreated, is something that you can't even fathom.

But it doesn't stop here. Prejudice ways exist in all facets. For instance, Islamophobia. In 2020, Europe banned the hijab in any corporate workplace. This started in Germany with some other countries following suit. Of course, this existed many years before: in France, 2011, women sitting in their burkinis on a beach, were removed because they covered up too much flesh. In 2004, France banned the wearing of hijabs and other visible religious symbols in state schools. Freedom countries, freedom of speech, freedom to wear what you want? Really?

There will always be that minority who will be what they are. I blame it on the lack of education. If you don't know or understand something, then you will say and conjure up what you think. Unconscious bias exists and there is a need to train and educate individuals so that this bias can be altered. And this is what is important: education, intermingling, let others understand your culture, what it's like to be you and walk in your shoes. Only then will people realise just how some are more privileged than others. Inclusion is so important.

Black Lives Matter

Black lives don't matter
All lives do
Said no one, besides a fool

It's the timeliness of the matter
That a certain life matters most
Of course, every life matters
But pick your timing to avoid confuse

Oppression, repression, digression
Are the self-servers tool
Cause hate amongst humanity
To fill your boots

The world needs help
Some more than others
If you can't be there in body
Then be there in good soul, sister or brother

We need to unite together
And stand up to the foes
For to be human, is to live
But most importantly, stand up for a cause

Colours of The Human Rainbow

If you tell me that you see no colour, just human
You may as well join the rest
For a view like this makes you a racist
I am sorry to attest

I may be brown, black or white
But of a colour I certainly am
Please look at my colour
And recognise me like that

I may be Christian, Muslim, Hindu, Jew or other
Please recognise my faith
Give me an identity
I really, really care

I may be binary, non or other
You can see me as that
See me as this label
Respect me, I certainly am that

For to disregard my identity
Is like ignoring any talent here
Recognise me. Accept me
We are all colours of the spectrum here

It›s this eclectic concoction
That gives the world its taste
We are seasons in the year
We are different grains in the sand
We are sunrise, sunset, dusk and dawn
We are the ephemeral souls
Passing through this lawn

The Hijab

A hijab is like wearing socks
It's part of the dress wear
A woman wears it not because she is oppressed
But because she feels free and proud and stronger everywhere

Europe nations, why such a narrow mindset you have
Seems like you've been cavorting, with the rule imposing nations
Made apparent with your rules, concocted of oppression
How does her scarf affect your peace-loving nation?

But then the penny drops
And I see what your plan is
Let's create more divide
For we are nothing but Islamophobic miscreants

A lady is harassed on the beach for her burkini
Being dragged like we were on the streets of Syria or Afghan living
Why is it offensive to wear more on the beaches
Your thinking seems to belong way back in the dark ages

Who will be next?
I wonder you see
Will it be Sikhs or the nuns?
Or anyone wearing a beard or rosary beads?

Will we need to don our hair in a certain way
Or will my tan be a shade that will throw some in disarray
Will the women have to wear heels and the men ties and cravats
For it seems like you've gone back fifty years, more or thrice

Europe nations, disappointing are you
I don't trust your strategy
You are just phobic of a belief
That has no place in your land, I conclude

Say Hell They Do

Black lives matter
Say hell they do!
George Floyd murdered
What am I supposed to do

IDF training
US cops' knee on the neck
Blood veins burning
With rage for the torment

Black people neglected
White colour supposedly the best
Black lives beneath you
White supremacy lives

Black slavery abolished
But what really has changed
US cops keeps ruling
Seeing things from an old lens

Cuckoo Klan disciples
Take off your horrible vests
Your colour doesn't define you
Your racism does the best

Oppression, depression
It has to end
Black Lives Matter!!
Right until the end

Football & Hooligans

Football hooliganism exists and there is an underlying reason for it. Fuelled by drink, inner turmoil, feelings of inadequacy, it's through hooliganism that a person can lash out and 'act hard'. The following words were written after and during the Euros 2020, which took place in 2021. It was disappointing to see what happened. England have had quite a reputation for it. But please note, a minority of yobs, does not represent the majority of fans…the real fans.

Then comes the racism– if you are a non-white player and doing great, then you are part of the team. If you are not, then you are ousted. Where is the loyalty? When Saka, Rashford and Sako all missed the penalties, the fans turned on them. A minority wrote hate speech, and it was devastating to read the comments and how racist the fans really were.

Then we had comedians, in particular one, who was cancelled after a racist remark about the players. Well done to his agent for making an example out of him and reiterating the importance of stating that 'racism will not be tolerated'.

England

England are in the finals
And some are feeling quite stressed
It's the aftermath from the minority
That usually causes disgrace

The England team need this
Southgate is doing great
But I can't speak for the fans or few
Where carnage will be leashed to grate

Booing a nine year old Viking and pulling another's hair
Spitting on some Danes. Really?
Even though it was an England win?
This really was quite cowardly, you balls of putrid hate

Barbarians, cavemen - with such low IQ and grace
Come on - stop with this pathetic hooligan way
Don't tarnish the reputation of TRUE England fans
Yes 'true' is what I say!!

That Chelsea Fan

A Chelsea fan stuck a flare up his nether regions
Thought he was a big man, famous
But he was nothing but an ignoramus
Then he made headlines
And he won't say sorry
It really is an attitude, you have to say so gory

He is looking forward to heading to Qatar in 2022
But what he doesn't know
Is that with acts like that
Just desserts will be due
Qatar isn't soft, like the UK's prime as minister
No tolerance for a wild animal, acting like a rotten as cadaver

He will be hearing the jingle jangle of keys
To a cell, if he's not careful
And will be pleading with the great Brits
To help him out, all of a sudden

So here is a message, Chelsea fan with the flare ass
Pop the bubble you are in
And pay pittance for your demeaning actions
Stop representing all of England
With your Neanderthal ways
And pay penance to such awful meanders,
that you so had to graze

It's Not Coming Home

England you played great
So saddened you lost
I sat anticipating. I felt sick after the draw
Then came extra time and penalties and we lost

But before, during and after
Bad energy was about
This led to the annihilation
So the England team went down

Outside the stadium in Wembley
Grown men got kicked about
Thugs tried hard to get in
Panicked the stewards, made them fraught

Zara stood in the stands
Wiping blood off her seat
As Mike had tried to stop a fight between fans
When Shaw had thrown one in

Buses had people jumping
Scaring the punters there in
Chants for the Italians sticking pasta somewhere
Was sung in tubes and transport within

Then when three of our good players missed the penalties
Abuse was hurled much so
Social media lit up with racism
It was disgusting, I tell you so

Boris you may denounce all this
But you are a poor leading example
England are renowned for its hooligans
But so not fans they are, it's boggling

This needs to be sorted
The attitude of these cretins
Else fifty-five years or so will pass
And we may never bring it home!!! It's stifling!

The Comedian [2]

There once was a silly comedian man
Ran out of material for his comedy and
So thought he'd exploit the game
Join the racist bigamists, what a shame
Only to be dealt with nothing, just egg on his face

Not so funny are you now
When venues don't want to smell you on their crowds
Your agent has walked away
You silly, racist
Not so funny pleb

Let's make you an example
Of mockery and 'won't stand for his babble'
Say no to hate and blame
Let's say no to racists
Let's put them to shame!!

---

[2] Inspired by the article: https://news.sky.com/story/comedian-andrew-lawrence-is-dropped-by-agent-after-racist-comments-in-the-wake-of-euro-2020-final-12354757

The Government

The title of this section should speak volumes. This is not only about the British government, (although it mostly is), but also touches on other countries.

In the UK, Boris Johnson[3], an Eton graduate and ex mayor of London, became prime minister. In his cabinet, he had a few ethnic minority individuals, who came to power under him. There is also another individual this book talks about: the then Health Secretary, Matt Hancock, who during the COVID crisis, stressed on the lockdown rules when he and others in the party, broke them so slyly. And then in 2022, the party gate scandal happened – where the work parties during lockdown were finally discovered. Whilst people stayed away from others and couldn't be by the bedside of their dying loved ones, Number 10 were up to all sorts, believing so naively that they wouldn't be caught out.

---

3 UK Prime Minister (2019 – 2022)

Also mentioned here is China, that continues the mistreatment of a certain minority. The plight of the Uighurs is a piece written to highlight and vent about the mistreatment of the Uighur people, an ethnic minority living in the Xinjiang region of China. Articles written by well known newspapers and accounts captured from actual Uighur people has been the source of this poem[4]. They are a punished people, kept in camps for some form of cleansing, where torture has been prevalent since 2016 or before.

Another person, infamous amongst some of the global world is the prime minister of India. Definitely no Gandhi, this man has been in the front page of the tabloids, where the Islamophobic bigotry that oozes from this leader and his Party has caused some to compare him to Hitler. If you are in the UK, the BBC Documentary: India, the Modi question, is a great insight into what happened back in 2002.

---

4 https://www.npr.org/2018/11/13/666287509/ex-detainee-describes-torture-in-chinas-xinjiang-re-education-camp

An Eton Mess

I've never liked an Eton mess
It's bitterly sweet, filling me with false believability
It's ingredients of the cabinet and prime minister Johnson
Has created such a state of indigestion

They swear by the wonderful messy structural state
So crumbled, that it's never so fulfilling as of late
Added with thick creamy lies
Responsible for where thousands of bodies lie

Not caring if they pile high up
As it's just another Eton mess, derriere up
But maybe it's time we opt for something delectable
Something more than just being a little palatable

Let's try something with more humane power
Something that will be agreeable, tastier and nothing lower
Not causing indigestion for you or me
For if not, an Eton mess will be all that we see

Plight of the Uighurs

Let's take a pause
Give the Uighurs a thought
Who will protest for them
Shout crimes of oppression and genocide on them
So many taken and hidden
In secret camps for supposed education
Taught a language, a life
Like a drug addict in rehabilitation

Made to pick cotton like it was 1802
Singing the national anthem
Before prayers and cultural celebrations are due
Can you imagine if 'Say, can you see'
Had to be sung before Thanksgiving dinner
Or if 'God save the queen'
Was to be heard before Christmas service, a christening or other.

Women sterilised
No more breeding o' you
So many heinous acts
I don't want to speak off
So crazy I tell you
Such a soul-less regime
What a dark lull of a dream

Oh United nations
Oh any humanitarian nation
Where are you now?
Please unite and help them, we bow
Come on Lowkey and other wordy artist
Please get together and awake your social media crowd list
Denounce such dictators
No different than Stalin, Netanyahu, Mugabe and Hitler

Mediocre fools
Wading in blood pools
Soul less, life less, perennial mules!
O' Qing rulers, you have lost what respect you have grown
You will be held responsible
For the ethnic cleansing you bestow
Communism may be your game
But in the end, love, faith and humanity will triumph once again

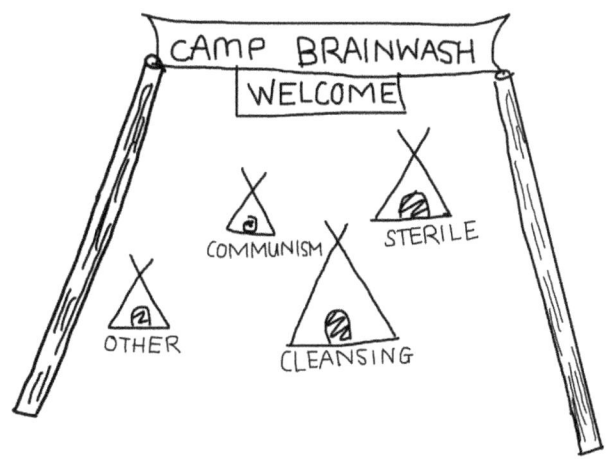

The Ruler of India

Oh India, dear India
What happened to you?
Your numbers hit the roof and gone so many of you
A year when it started
The Muslims were castrated
For holding a gathering, when the virus was burning
Reality of course
Scapegoats were just of want
And now just recently
Festivals held in front
Dipping in the river
All things collided
And look what came out of it
So many dead bodies burning
Breadwinners disappearing
Widows and orphans made
Survival the hardest
So many, many displaced
Whilst of course, the man leading
Seems to want the winnings in all a place
Care or care not, something needs to be replaced

The Straw Man

There was a man in charge of an island
An Island that tried to conquer the world
A man in charge, whose words are a risk
To the Island and its woes

He wants to wait for bodies to pile up
Before the island is again locked up
This man is clearly culpable
Of what he has avowed

The man with a golden mop of hair
Who sat on his laurels when a bat virus came to town
A man worshipped by the rich or some
And loathed by so many more

An Etonian
A bike man
A ludicrous has been
The man must go

And therefore it is a country's insanity
To forsake the risk to humanity
If the man in charge
Rules for many more

The Misfits

Our dear Prime Minister
Has questions to be answered
About a certain hypocrisy
He recently endeavoured

Practise what you preach
Has never been in his cabinet's book of belief
But now it has them all in a fix
As certain veracity has been leaked

How atrocious was it back in May(5)
When people were locked down in their homes again
With dear souls in pain and suffering
Full of distraught, hurt and heartbreak they were feeling

And families couldn't be by the bedsides
Of their dearest loved ones that were dying
And the departees couldn't say bye
Only surrounded by NHS strangers, for their end of care life

But rules are rules, said these fools
And so, the public and the Queen abided
With the Nazi camp likeness, set up so defiantly
That the government had so well been devising

---
5 May 2021

But quietly creeping at the house at Number 10
There were gatherings, of work meetings, they excusably said
With the room filled with ministry dreads
Where drinks had to be served, in so much red

For not drinking on the job was not ever heard of
Then came the cheese and crackers and some other smorgasbord
Maybe some music - you know the ministry had some moves
Twerking and grinding - they're so good at, there is proof

So many things to be accountable for
But squirming out of this hole,
you have so much experience, right Bo
Never ever a question answered directly
More like swirling round with words, it's so cowardly

Oh well, the people are awake
As more and more parties are dug up from the grave
But what's next, will there be a wake
Unbelievable disrespect of the people,
from these misfit Tory heads

Film & Media

The film and media world are not 'what you see is what you get'. The illusion that you finally see, involves a multitude of tasks that are executed by a plethora of talent. The crew, actors, producers, directors, catering staff, cleaners and so many more, are the ones who transport you to the finished product. And just as 'WOW' the visuals, just as 'OMG' are some of the behind-the-scenes activities.

However, as enticing as this may all appear, there is an unspeakable underlying tone about the cruelty of crew members and the seediness of the execs. The crew often work a crazy number of hours. They go without sleep and sometimes not even food, exhausted by working crazy hours. Then there are the predators. fuelled by power, greed and an animalistic urge. Believing they are invincible, these vultures forget that they're just made of flesh and their seedy perverted activities will come and bite them in the ass.

And that is the Film and Media industry. Bright, yet dark. Attractive yet ugly. Seductive, yet repulsing.

Film Crew Cruelty

Sad and disgusted at what entertains me usually
Films and series, I adore so neatly
But what goes on in the background, I was never known to
It's worse than animals being held in some cocoon

It takes a tribe to make a movie
Not just director, producer, actor or exec lady
What about the crew that run around all day
Did you know they work more than a nurse on a pandemic stay

Lack of sleep can lead to their fatality
I don't care if you are pregnant, puke in the bin. Do you hear me!?
Was told an editor in the edit room, so grimly
Cruelty to humans! Is this the entertainment industry?

Things need to change. The best need to get better
Reign in on the bullying naysayers
Maybe women need to take the lead
There will be more empathy. Just maybe

The Wine Stone

Man o' philistine
Satan in disguise
Repulsed the women
Who were left in his demise

Power took over that seedy mind
Thought he had power
Than the universe
The man with no spine

Owning studios
Too much money
Made him invincible
In his tarnished mind

And it only took one
To tell this secret so
And that's when others shouted
Me too, me too and more

Me Too

He worked at the Vic Hall
And tried it on with all the boys
Called them to his room
Tried to lure them, what a mule

Then his show got cancelled
House of cards or something other
He was a Kaiser kind of sorts
What kind of man, preying on all sorts

Definitely the usual suspect
Brought to reveal after the 'Me Too' campaign
It's so underwhelming
For us fans who for you, were rooting
Now we sit here and scowl, only in disdain

Oops

A film about a run
For accidental shooting with a gun
Has two boys in despair
Shot in New Mexico, so the scenes can be great

But never has irony been so cruel
For the film in real life, became true
A sad, unfortunate, heart breaking unfold
As the talented cinematographer came to know

Shot with a prop, was her demise
How could such a fatality happen, not wise
Or was more involved?
Just like the case with Brandon Lee, once upon a time

Who do we blame?
For such careless misgivings
Who was the expert and safety there?
Or were these mishaps just common

A life gone, a man injured
A crew scared and treated unfair
Had to walk out, whilst that beautiful soul bared
Left her loved ones so broken, so in despair
This reality is not right. This needs to be repaired

The Pied Piper

A predator sits on trial
He thought he could fly
He thought age was nothing but a number
His just deserts are being served, oh so cold

His minions tried to silence the mass
But the truth could not be suppressed
A sociopath, a psychopath, a serial abuser
Unpunished you went, for so long

And now you sit there
What thoughts run through that dark soul
Do you feel remorse?
Or do you first need to know the wrongdoings you imposed?

Was it daddy issues that made you so?
Or was it fame and the power
You weren't smart enough to endure?
What turns a man into a wild animal

But calling you an animal, is being tame
A rabid dog, is what you were with fame
So here you are
It's all bumps in the new grind

That will be your future now
You may get a slither of what is due
But your true desserts will be served
Much so in the afterlife we accrue

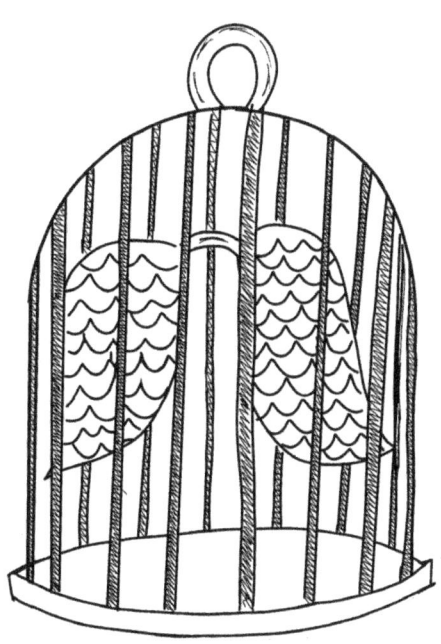

Digital Addiction & Suffering

There is a serious problem that needs to be addressed. There is an addiction out there and it is not to do with drink, drugs, gambling or anything else we know so common. It's a digital addiction.

Technology is innovating rapidly, from phones to tablets to the social media world. Information is available within a millisecond. The Text Neck Syndrome, a term coined to describe the posture formed from leaning forward to look down at your phone, as we spend copious amounts of time to text, scroll and view, is prevalent amongst many. We are drawn into this world with our devices, not even realising how much of our time, body, mind and soul gets consumed. But this is not only the price. This also affects relationships, self esteem and security.

Then there is the Flex Culture, which is destroying the masses, as they live hand to mouth, paycheck to paycheck, just so that they can pull in the crowds and build their image, flexing through the social media world. Another addiction prevalent within the digital world is that within the gaming world. The poem written about this, touches on true events that have occurred in the world. None of what I have included, has been made up.

And who is responsible for some of these addictions? The big media establishments that provide the platform. Inspired by the documentary: The Social Dilemma, 'Social Media Wizardry' tells of the exploitation of the people by the Social media predators, not caring about the impact on its users, all for the goal of making more billions.

And it's because of these addictions, just like drug rehabilitation, there exist rehab centers and retreats, that help individuals overcome this type of addiction, in order to lead a normal happy life. Digital rehabilitation.

Flex

Buy my Jordans
Put my Balmains on
Get a pic for the gram
Let's impress the boys and girls

Been grafting at the gym
Got my body ripped and firing
Bought a new car
It's sexy than what Musk or Bezos drive in

Put it on Tik Tok
Tweets and Snaps all in
Need to let the people know
I don't care about the money, I'm not saving

Though need to put the extra hours in
For this costly world affair
But priceless it so is
For my status and street cred – laissez faire

Yes, it's a fulltime workout
Heavy on my mind and my near non existent bank balance
But I need them so impressed
It's all about the low key, high key flex!

For the Gram

Makeup on right or biceps pumped up high
You look like you are a drag queen - why?
It's for the Gram
I'm an influencer - part time

Have to fuel my followers
Have to put a high in my bloodstream
It's like a caffeine fix
But do you know, I also get paid to do this

Some days are good, some days are bad
When a one thousand likes only make me feel poor, it's a fact
It's twenty thousand or more, that my heart desires
It's an addict's intuition, what comes and goes

And it's a costly old game
Paying pittance for a little ounce of fame
When the trolling commences
My armour comes grating
Words can be like knives or petals entwined
Making me high or sometimes so unrefined
It's a cycle of feelings
One hit, one hit and sometimes a blow

This is my world
A digital concoction of feelings
Reeling, wheeling for the next hit and more
It's what us influencers have to endure

Text Neck Syndrome

My eyes are open
But I'm in soft slumber
Eyes down in dreamland
I swipe scroll and wonder

A second turns to a minute
A minute to an hour
I look up and think darn
But look down, just five minutes or other

Media on my phone
I cannot put it down
It pulls me more and more
I cannot get enough, I tremble

My phone is like a ligament
Social media, my membrane
Head down, neck bent
I have the Text Neck Syndrome

A Gamers Life

I'm in a bad mood today
Got to get my console out
Play until dawn hits the cloud
Then I can sleep til' the world is up and out

I don't play all day that often
Only during school hours
And then way after lights go out
It's all part of the mission

Keep keeping the score
Play with your virtual mates
In another world
I so love to render

Mum says I need permission
Dad wants me in some rehab admission
But this is just my hobby
Like reading, writing or some football story

I don't wear a nappy
Like some gamers do
So, they don't have to go walk elsewhere
To relieve themselves of those fluids they fuelled

I am also not some guy in Japan
Who had his leg amputated
Got D.V.T from all the non moving
When he could not pause from the game he was playing

Or what about the couple in Korea
Who fed their virtual baby more than their own
Killing that poor kid of lack of nutrition
Whilst their V.R. one thrives, full of fruition

So yes, I am just a gamer
No crazy addict you know
I just play my games for escapism
It's what gets me through and through

Digital Addiction

Minutes turn to hours
Hours into days
A lot of life is left, dreaming awake
Lost in scrolling, posting, hoping ways

Dopamine hits from likes, not workouts
Serotonin from comments good, not burnouts
This is the world, lured and set in our brain
This is the social media, new age

So much effort, just for the gram
Painted faces, just for the hits and likes - don't frown
Pictures enhanced, look at my life so polished
Let's turn the eaten bit of the apple, away from the likers

Then come the haters, comments so worse
Why not enough likes, I don't understand you all
Scrolling my posts, not liking it at all
Anger enraged, within some of the veteran addicts you know

Dopamine replaced with anxiety
Sadness, depression and insecurity
Engrossed with why and what could have been
Let's check again and again, in case it could not be

Social media addiction - it is real, it exists
Too much time spent digitally, sends reality flying by so quick
Too much of this and that, is never good for the soul
Let's find a balance, let's not let it take our control

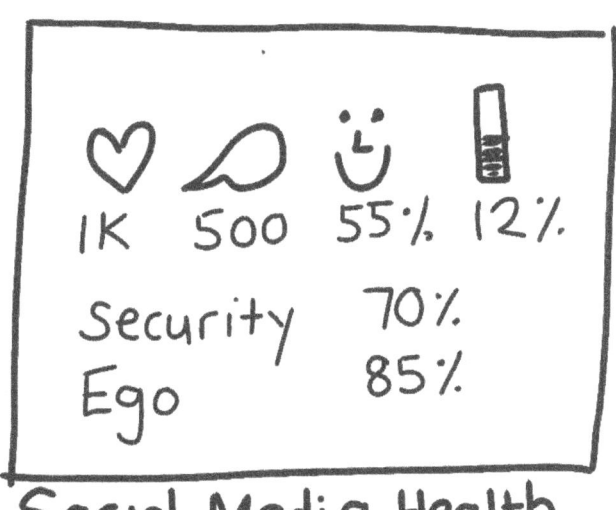

Social Media Wizardry

Click on an ad or post
Then see the magic unfold
Every time you scroll your page
Get transfixed on some informational fix

This is how social media and the ad world pile up the wealth
With smart stalking of every step you take
The digital world knows how to draw you in on the take
A take that costs you time and your mental health

Algorithms set and clever tricks up ahead
This is the social media world, doing its best
Pulling you in like a candy stick for a kid
Knowing that this post or ad, you will definitely click

And then what happens?
You become some digital addict
Drawing yourself into this world
So different from reality

Not paying attention to
What's I.R.L blatantly
This is what you call
The world of Social Media Wizardry

Rehab

They told me I had to go to rehab
I asked: Is this a joke?
I'm no drug addict or alcoholic
Nor a gambler just a little food addict

They told me that it had gone too far
My supposed invisible addiction
You can't see it? It was a request
I have no idea, I stressed

So, rehab I got to
And then the penny dropped
All the digital gadgets
Were taken and so easily locked up

Then I really felt the pangs
My hands needed something to hold
My mind was running like an athlete
Whilst my heart's vessel was ready to burst

I had a million things to browse, to swipe
To text, comment on and like
I had FOMO and YOLO
I could not breathe. I was in deep

Then it hit me. Was this my addiction really?
I could not believe my tragedy
Rehab was surely working
As my digital addiction blared into reality

Climate
Catastrophe

We are killing the world. We are destroying its essence. Whilst the big global companies continue to produce huge amounts of waste, emitting gases into the air and excreting waste into the sea and on the ground, then this is a problem that will worsen through time. We have eight years[6] to reverse the climate catastrophe that is upon us. People need to be educated and induced with a thought process that will allow them to understand how to use and create waste effectively.

Then there are the clothes company and one in particular that I refer to, that produce vast amounts of clothing. Using clever copycatting and algorithms to pull in the masses, it is one of the biggest producers of clothes waste, causing the shopaholic in its customers. Success driven by algorithms, similar to what Facebook has done, the goods produced by this shrewd Chinese company are no different to the fake, branded products that are sold in a fish market. You can even smell the fishiness of this all from right here.

---

6 Stated in 2022

Climate Change

The earth, she is catching her breath
She's finding difficulty in breathing
Her lungs have been tarnished with human destruction and pain
The days of bloom, she is yearning

Fires burn enormously in the Amazon
She can feel it in her veins
Too much CO_2 emissions have been released
It's not helping the earth cells to embrace

Her children have been defiant
Ruining her demeanour and all
Throwing wastage into her waters
Causing malnourishment within her throws

Detonation being released
That leave tremors within her soul
Her children elsewhere feel her pain
And destruction falls upon them with huge sorrow

Her temperature rises
Like a fever, so highly strong
She's getting warmer, then hotter
It's her demise, we contribute to too much so

The earth she is catching her breath
She's finding difficulty in breathing
What have we done to our world
We must stand up to our duty

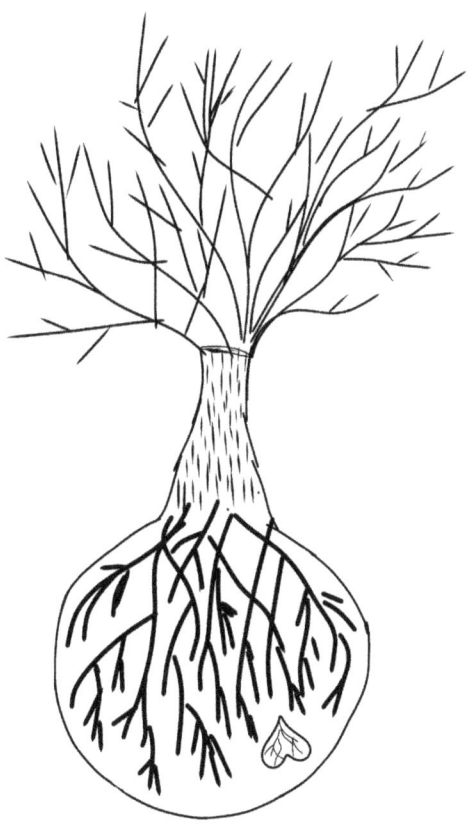

Shopaholic

The addict quenches her fix
Fingertips tapping and scrolling so lit
Feeling the high as items added to the basket
It's so cheap, I'll add more she thinks

The China dealer provides her, her hit
So pleasing, they add her money to the mills
Millions more quench their fix
So high, until high needs another hit

These are the clothing companies exploiting all the world
Helping the addicts with their find and their fix
In such clever planned and created outfits
They're no different than some other product dealing misfit

Using media, to draw in the punters
Clever programming, to conjure what was glanced at
Competition, it's at the top
Copying others' garments liked, but at low money you know

Workers it owns, exploited
Racism, prejudice, no Uighurs - it's points in
Cares so not for the environment cacophony
Only about building its own economy

More garments worn
More garments thrown
Added to the earthly waste pile
Not small

No help towards the care of the climate, it's gross
Just embezzling millions with their laws
From brainwashed humans
It's oh so raw

Recycle Freecycle

You put one can here
The food scraps over there
Keep clear of the plastics
Or they will be recycled back in your intestinal wear

Yes, plastics in the sea
In the belly of a fish
Catch, wash, and cook
It's back like karma in your body

Recycle, freecycle, it's all so important in reality
You aren't free from it
Even if you are a privileged soul
I tell you and me

What have we done to this world?
What have we done?
Remember the MJ song
Yes what have we done?!

We've got it heating up
And being a drama queen
With so many over exaggerated
Flood, fire and quaky emotions

It's so important to prevent the waste
Else landfills will swell where we inhabitants dwell
And the world will change so rapidly
That adjusting to it will be hell

The Eejits

An Irish term for an idiot, there are plenty of eejits about in this world, from government bodies, the wealthiest, to the Z listers. There's not much else to say about these types of people, besides an Eejit is not always defined by lack of intelligence, as some of the individuals mentioned, are highly smart, intellectual sorts, ranging from Etonian grads to the wealthiest men on earth. It's the idiotic decisions, actions and shrewd manoeuvres that makes one an Eejit here.

This section will touch on the wealthy tax avoiders, who dodged the federal tax income, as revealed through the investigation carried out by ProPublica. All, whilst regular people came home with a pay packet enough to feed the kids only.

Another Eejit talked of here is no other than the UK's home secretary[7]. Born to immigrant parents herself, she has had a hypocritical air about her, who classes immigrants as foreign criminals, disagrees with the freedom of movement and has fraternised with the enemy. Not only is she a hardcore Brexiteerr and very much anti-immigration, she has also been pro death penalty which she later backtracked about. (And since this book is being published in 2023, you could easily replace her name with the current brave-man who has built a huge enemy base just from the words she has regurgitated. Insulting culture, creed and humanity in general.)

And then we have Boris, the then prime minister of the UK himself. Educated in one of the top schools and universities, but just like his demeanour, he has projected a comical ruling in the country, and has ended up disgruntling a lot of the citizens.

---

7 Priti Patel

Cock O' Han

Hancock, really you lived up to your name
You preached a belief not in your name
You and Judas would go hand in hand
You swapped germs and gave them to your loved ones

Now I know your private life is none of our business
But hypocrisy done, is a huge 'duped us' nuisance
Your false words and talk, were acted well
But we will never believe another word, you utter or put on us to dwell

But it doesn't get better, some say it may be even worse
Bringing that finance man in to take your hearse
A man who has openly denied his roots and existence
Wants to be a white man. when his roots were brown, we know long once

Yes, that Javid is a mutton, dressed as lamb
Just another puppet, in this bureaucracy of hell
But it won't be surprising if Cock o' Han is back
Isn't that what happens with these government cats

The Witch of the UK

Priti Patel[8]
Sold the devil her soul
A token brown puppet
For Bojo to devour

Forgot her roots
And where she came from
When only from Uganda
Came her dear migrant parents

A tyrant she is
No different from dictators
With a name so given
That so doesn't serve her

An iced cold soul
Bathing in hypocritical oaths
The not so Priti Patel
Has been feckless in her talk

No conscience for the dead
Or how migrants should be dealt
The Satan got her in bed
That's the not so Priti Patel

---

8 2022 had Suella Braverman. The name can be replaced with this person also.

Katie Hopkins

Katie Hopkins
Pudding and Pie
Annoyed everyone
And made them cry

Racist. Prejudice, crazy maid
With no sensitivity
Of what she says in disdain

Her words, like puking bile
Smelly repugnant enough
To want to run a mile

Hair like Boris
Or Worzel Gummidge
Katie Hopkins
You are so full of rubbish!!

Rwanda

Patel, she's been strategising
She has her broom out
She's cleaning
Sending people to a place in Africa
Rwanda is where it's all going to be at

It feels so unethical, so not humane
Rwanda is no American dream
It sounds like a safe place to live
But what goes behind the scenes
You need to read in

How about your ancestors Patel?
Should they have been carted too?
Get you to Rwanda
Yes, you lot from Uganda
There's no room at the Inn here

I don't care how much of the tax we use up
This must be actioned, it's a serious clean up
Is this charity as they say?
Or is this a politician usual
"Let them think we are doing great favour on them"

The Robbers

The wealthiest of men, stole from the state
To feed their hollow soul,
that they've been struggling with therein

Held so high in regard, with their wisdom and words
It broke the world's heart,
when learning of their tax nonexistence

How can three men's wealth equal fifty percent
of the poorest wealth
How can twenty-five individuals have a wealth
equalling one point one trillion

This is what you call the inequality income
This is what you call a perfect worldly imbalance

Where flying to space, is an activity at your disposal
Where a word you utter can cause shares to tumble

So, these powerful men, like magicians,
have stolen from the globe
Not paying any tax, like the mere hardworking individuals

This nonsensical fact, baffles all to the last drop
And reinforces the perfect income inequality and
economical imbalance

Sunak & Will Smith

It's funny when a politician
Compares the Will Smith saga to his own
Explaining he knows what it's like
When your wife is being joked off

No, no Sunak, that is so different
Just like Sumak is a herb and Susuk a sausage
Your wife is avoiding tax
Not losing her eyebrows

You put the tax up for the mere working class
Making us poorer as we scrimp for the last payment
I don't care if she's a non dom and her daddy a billionaire
If she lives here for years, pay up, don't be square!!

You see the Tory farce, continues on immensely
From party gate, virus strategy, Hancock and other debacles
So settle in people, get the popcorn and drinks out
Let's see what else unfolds and provides circus like entertainment

The People

A topic that pulls at the heart strings and a cause that needs to be addressed. This section touches on first world poverty, refugees, war and an imbalance in the world.

Child poverty in the UK is at its worst, even more so after the pandemic. The poor are getting poorer. Children are turning up to schools hungry and cold. Over 130,000 children out of 400,000 are homeless in the UK with 4.3 million[9] living in poverty. Mothers are scrimping on food so that they can provide for their children instead. Charity starts on your home turf. Marcus Rashford has done a lot for this area and hats off to him, but it's just not enough. The Children's Society are a charity doing a lot to help. You can read more and donate to them here https://www.childrenssociety.org.uk/how-you-can-help/donate/where-your-money-goes

Then we have the elite, the richest dodging tax because they made losses that year. If the working class get taxed or have the universal credit cut, then how is it that the rich can get away with using what's due, to wipes their asses instead. Or devour a steak costing 1000 dollars because it is flaked with 24 carat gold, which will eventually be expelled from the human body anyway.

---

9 Data from 2020

And then let's not forget the refugees, who escape their war torn countries risking their own lives and that of loved ones, to get to a place of some peace. Only to find that the green grassed land isn't as emerald as it may seem and that the dwellers aren't so welcoming of the potential settlers.

The Doomed Children

There are thousands of children homeless in the UK
So, let's start with charity right on our doorstep
Turning up to school, starved and empty
Let's put our hearts and soul in helping our own

There are thousands of children deprived in the UK
Turning up to school with clothes torn and winter coats needed
Shoes all altered. Socks so holy
Let's stitch up their tiny souls. Put a smile on their face

There are thousands of children treated badly in the UK
Turning up to school, homework not done, looking tired and angry
Mother with her new boyfriend, so siblings needed looking after
I want to be a drug dealer, just like my daddy

There are thousands of children yearning for help in the UK
Coming to learn, for it's their only happiest place
With teachers who care, teachers who help
Breakfast served to fill with warmth, and lots of care to make them feel safe

This is the state of the UK childcare system
A developed country where no soul should be hungry
A developed country where no tiny human should be freezing
A developed country where no child should be homeless

Eating Cereal

She's eating cereal for her dinner
So her daughter doesn't go without
This is the state of a first world nation
Where families are left with naught

Poverty is at its highest
Starvation, deprivation in mounts
This is the working-class status
These are families in a drought

A homeless man sits at the corner
Begging for change you can give
It's not always to feed a drug habit or drink
It's to feed that empty stomach within

State funds only stretch so much
Two slices of bread, an apple, maybe more
Christmas looks bleak for many yonder
Where children are gifted winter coats

Food banks fill to the brim
Energy bills soar, so let's scrimp
Where switching on heat from a device
Is a common person's dream

This is the state of a first world nation
Where imbalance spreads like fire
This is the state of a first world nation
Where quality living is dire

The Imbalance

John sat in his cosy slippers
There's a wind howling outside
Let's add more wood to the burner
Let's devour this hot chocolate inside

We have made it almost my love
Amar smiles at his wife
Just a little more on this rubber boat
And we will be free of the tyranny we had

A better life to be had
No poverty or war
No dictator to tell us what more
My love, my life, we will all live in peace and harmony

Not a good day to be at sea
John wonders what those fishermen will be feeling
Up and down that channel
How tormenting must be that feeling

Up and down this boat we go
Oh dear UK, here we come
The weather is getting worse
But hope we hold on to, to make it through

Twenty-seven souls killed whilst crossing the sea
The fishermen indeed had a challenging day
Not by weather but by the cemetery they saw
Read John, the news about the channel they frequently knew

So many people dying
To live a dream they think is real
A better life than the hell they once lived in
This is their reality, our real world

Nations from each side of the channel
Don't wash your hypocritical hands
Find those smugglers if you do care
And help these migrants, they are just like you and me. Humans!

Two Sides of the Spectrum

A child in Africa stands with pangs
Pangs of hunger that swell his midriff
Poverty soaks so many in this world
Third world, first world
Starvation, what has gone amiss?

A man snuffs a steak, flecked with twenty-four carat gold
Social media on fire of some man sprinkling salt
That piece of cow that costs more than one's yearly intake
So much craze for twenty minutes of divulge
The world has gone crazy over some meat
that will only be expunged

There is so much imbalance here.
One extreme to another
From starvation, desperation to self-indulgent big spenders
No care, guilt or thought, on what is happening on earth
It's more important to grab a shot for the gram or
social media worth.

Let's not forget all children of this world
The ones with smiles and bellies filled with love
Let's not forget that overindulgence
cannot be great for you and me
It can make one desensitised
It's our very own worst enemy

Armistice Day

When Archduke Franz Ferdinand got shot by the Serbs
The Austro-Hungarian tribe decided to burst
And the Russians joined the Serbs, also allied by the French
And the rest was a domino effect where other nations made their bed

How many died? Nine million and more
What a waste of life. For what exactly? Such gore
The lands destroyed with death, grew a weed soaked in red
Blood on its petals, the poppy was what it was named

It's Armistice Day today. Remembering those who died
Who fought, who got wounded, who were left to normalise
Lives taken so early - all for an ego led war
Then came the second one, the worst to end all wars

*Thank you for reading.
Let's make a difference, let's show the world we care.*

www.ingramcontent.com/pod-product-compliance
Lightning Source LLC
Chambersburg PA
CBHW061749070526
44585CB00025B/2844